The author wishes to thank the photographers and photo agencies who contributed the photographs (all under copyright) to this book:

Magnum Photos/Abbas p. 10 left, Richard Klavar p. 1, Eric Lessing p. 14, Wayne Miller p. 9, Marilyn Silverstone p. 21, Dennis Stock p. 17; Nancy Sheehan p. 26; SuperStock, Inc./Scott Barrow p. 29, Kurt Scholz p. 23, Ned Valentin p. 27 top; Valan Photos/John Eastcott & Yva Momatiuk p. 7, Val & Alan Wilkinson p. 13; Viesti Associates/Michael Lewis p. 8 right, 11, Craig Lovell p. 16, Eleni Mylonas p. 5, 22, Joe Viesti back cover, Edward G. Young p. 28; Woodfin Camp & Associates/Alexandria Avakian p. 25, Bernard Boutrit front cover, David Burnett p. 4, John Eastcott & Yva Momatiuk p. 6, 10 right, 24, 27 bottom, Chuck Fishman p. 2, Kal Muller p. 15, A. Reiniger p. 8 left, Israel Talby p. 12, 18, 19, 20.

Printed in the United States of America
First Edition   1 2 3 4 5 6 7 8 9 10
Library of Congress Cataloging in Publication Data
Morris, Ann. Weddings / by Ann Morris.
   p.   cm. Summary: A picture book provides a simple introduction to the things that often happen at a wedding.
ISBN 0-688-13272-3. — ISBN 0-688-13273-1 (lib. bdg.) 1. Marriage customs and rites—Juvenile literature.
[1. Marriage customs and rites. 2. Weddings.] I. Title.
GT2665.M65 1995 391.5—dc20 94-48040 CIP AC(CIP)

ANN MORRIS

WEDDINGS

LOTHROP, LEE & SHEPARD BOOKS

NEW YORK

4

All over the world, a wedding is a very special celebration.

It is the time when a man and a woman promise to spend the rest of their lives together.

Weddings can be plain or fancy . . .

indoors or outdoors . . .

but they are always special occasions.

Family and friends want to be there.

Everyone dresses up —

15

especially the bride and groom.

Here come the bride and groom —on foot,

in a car,

or a boat,

even on an elephant!

The bride and groom promise to love and care
for each other always.

They may say a prayer together.

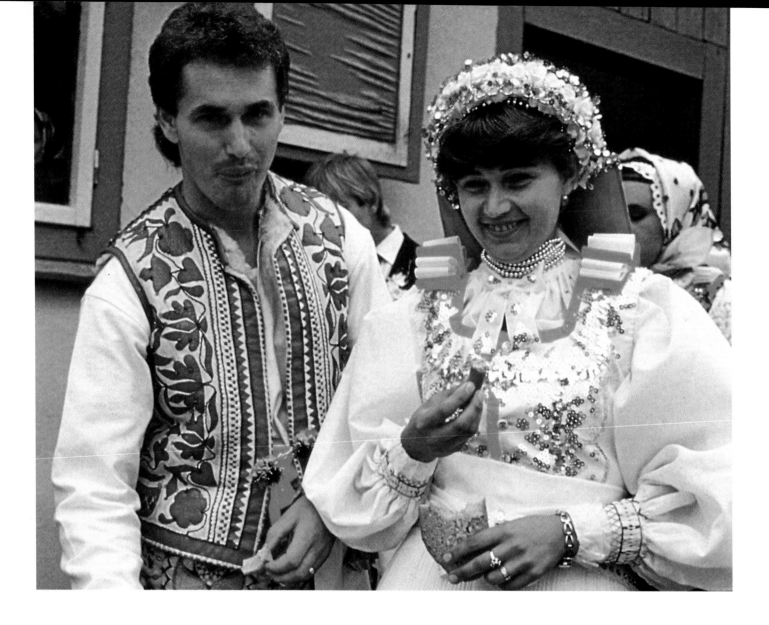

or share a special food.

Sometimes they exchange rings or a kiss.

After the ceremony, there is food and music and dancing.

Often there are gifts for the bride and groom. Always there are everyone's wishes for a long and happy life together.

INDEX

15 INDONESIA: Attendants cool the bride and groom with fans during a wedding on tropical Sumbawa Island.

16 INDIA: This Kashmiri bride and groom wear necklaces of money to show that they can afford to be married and take on the responsibilities of family life.

17 GHANA: Many Moslems believe it is proper to cover the head in public. The modest bride is veiled from head to toe.

18 SOUTH AFRICA: A bright flock of bridesmaids and a flower girl escort a wedding couple to church.

19 JAPAN: This bride is wearing a style of dress that is centuries old to be married in a Shinto rite at Heian Shrine in Kyoto.

20 SWEDEN: A church boat ferries the bride across Lake Siljan to her wedding.

21 INDIA: A bride is carried in a palanquin through the streets of Jaipur. The groom follows, riding an elephant.

22 INDIA: The dot of red powder on this Hindu bride's forehead is called a *kumkum*.

23 THAILAND: A Bangkok couple are linked by a strand of yarn during their wedding to symbolize how love binds them together.

24 SLOVAKIA: The traditional wedding meal for a Slovak bride and groom is sausages, which are supposed to bring them many children.

25 RUSSIA: This Jewish couple wear rings to remind them of their marriage vows. A wedding ring is usually worn on the third finger of the left hand.

26 UNITED STATES: A bride dances with her flower girls.

27 IRAN: Everyone dances at a wedding!

27 SLOVAKIA: Passersby stop to watch as Gypsy musicians lead a wedding procession through the streets.

28 UNITED STATES: Family and friends bring gifts to help this Navaho bride and groom furnish their first home.

29 UNITED STATES: Throwing rice at the newlyweds is a way to wish them a long, happy life together and many children.

Where in the world were these photographs taken?

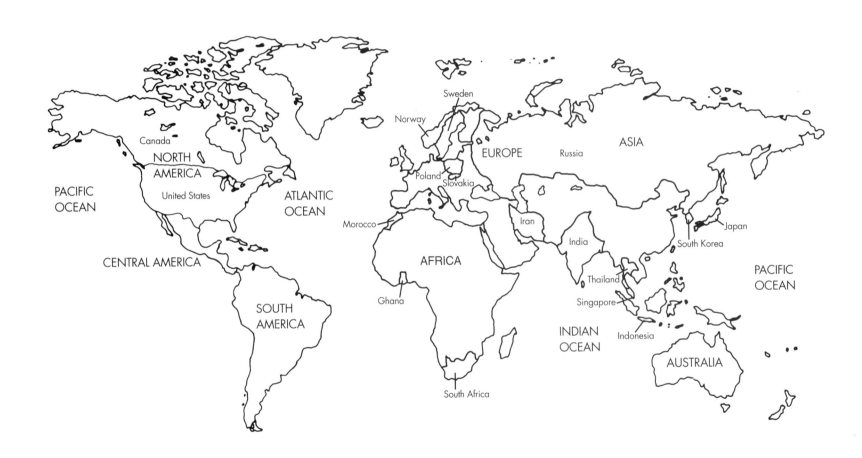